THE LITTLE
BOOK
ABOUT
GOD

ron rhodes

HARVEST HOUSE PUBLISHERS
EUGENE, OREGON

THE LITTLE BOOK ABOUT GOD
Copyright © 2013 by Ron Rhodes
Published by Harvest House Publishers
Eugene, Oregon 97402
www.harvesthousepublishers.com

ISBN 978-0-7369-5185-2 (hardcover)
ISBN 978-0-7369-5186-9 (eBook)

Printed in China

13 14 15 16 17 18 19 20 21 / FC-CD / 10 9 8 7 6 5 4 3 2 1

Contents

INTRODUCTION

Thank you for your interest in this book! I pray that even though it is a little book, it will bring a big blessing to your life. It is uniquely formatted...

- ▶ Each chapter is short—just two pages.

- ▶ Each chapter begins by stating the big idea.

- ▶ This is followed by bullet points that concisely expand on the big idea, with Bible references.

- ▶ I then quote a few of the very best Bible verses that illustrate the big idea.

- ▶ On the second page of each chapter, I provide "fast facts" that relate to the big idea.

- ▶ Each chapter closes with some applications—"truths that transform"—and a thoughtful quote from a recent or not-so-recent Christian leader.

This abbreviated format allows for maximum information in minimal space. This is a little book, but it contains lots of information. Feel free to look up some of the verses I cite. That will greatly enrich your study.

Here's an added benefit of the book. Because it contains 28 chapters, it is ideally suited for four weeks of brief daily devotionals on the doctrine of God.

The Purple Color of This Book

The purple color of this little book is significant. It is intended to reflect the royal and regal nature of our true King, God Almighty. God is the "King of the ages" (1 Timothy 1:17), the "great king over all the earth" (Psalm 47:2). He is truly the "King of kings" (1 Timothy 6:15).

Illumination Through Prayer

I suggest that you begin each chapter with a short prayer. Ask God to open your spiritual eyes of understanding so that you can fully grasp what He wants you to understand. The psalmist set a great example for us. He prayed: "Open my eyes, that I may behold wondrous things out of your law" (Psalm 119:18). The Holy Spirit delights in illumining our minds to spiritual truths (1 Corinthians 2:10-11).

Anticipate Spiritual Blessing

As you learn more about God, expect to be blessed spiritually. Remember that Bible study is not just about head apprehension, it's also about life-transforming heart appropriation (see Romans 12:2). Of course, we must be willing to submit ourselves to Scripture for this to occur. As Scripture puts it, we must be doers of the Word, and not just hearers (James 1:22). Doers of the Word experience the blessings of the Word (Psalm 1)!

Reasons to Believe in God

THE BIG IDEA

God is not a fairy tale character. A number of convincing philosophical arguments provide rational support for God's existence.

What You Need to Know

- ▶ The *cosmological* argument says that every effect must have an adequate cause. The existence of the universe is an effect that must have been caused by God.

- ▶ The *teleological* argument notes that there is an obvious purposeful design of the world and universe. The Designer must be God.

- ▶ The *moral* argument says every human being has an innate sense of moral obligation. Where did it come from? It must have been God.

Verses to Contemplate

"Every house is built by someone, but the builder of all things is God" (Hebrews 3:4).

"The heavens declare the glory of God" (Psalm 19:1).

"His invisible attributes, namely, his eternal power and divine nature, have been clearly perceived, ever since the creation of the world" (Romans 1:20).

Truths That Transform

1. Because there is a Creator-God, you and I as creatures are responsible to obey Him (Psalm 119:2,44-45,60,100,112).

2. We are called to obey with our whole hearts (Joshua 24:14-15; Romans 6:17-18).

3. Obedience brings God's blessing (Psalm 1). Disobedience, however, brings God's hand of discipline (Hebrews 12:5-11).

4. Obedience also yields happiness (Psalm 119:56).

A Quote to Ponder

"If the universe had not been made with the most exacting precision we could never have come into existence. It is my view that these circumstances indicate the universe was created for man to live in."

Robert Jastrow

2

God Is a Revealer

THE BIG IDEA

God has always taken the initiative to reveal Himself to humankind.

What You Need to Know

- ▶ There are two primary ways God has revealed Himself.

- ▶ *General revelation* refers to the ways God has communicated to all persons of all times. An example is God's revelation of Himself in the world of nature (Psalm 19; Romans 1:20).

- ▶ *Special revelation* refers to God's specific and clear way of speaking through His mighty acts in history, the person of Jesus Christ, and the prophets and apostles (whose writings are in the Bible).

Verses to Contemplate

"Long ago, at many times and in many ways, God spoke to our fathers by the prophets, but in these last days he has spoken to us by his Son" (Hebrews 1:1-2).

"When the Spirit of truth comes, he will guide you into all the truth, for he will not speak on his own authority, but whatever he hears he will speak, and he will declare to you the things that are to come" (John 16:13).

FAST FACTS
Christ Revealed...

God's awesome power (John 3:2)

God's incredible wisdom (1 Corinthians 1:24)

God's boundless love (1 John 3:16)

God's unfathomable grace (2 Thessalonians 1:12)

Truths That Transform

1. The word "communication" brings to mind someone telling us about himself—telling us what he knows, opening up his mind to us, asking for our attention, and seeking a response.
2. That is what divine revelation is all about. God does this through the Bible (2 Peter 1:21).
3. Rejoice that God speaks to you through the pages of the Bible (2 Timothy 3:15-17).

A Quote to Ponder

"[The Bible is] God preaching, God talking, God telling, God instructing, God setting before us the right way to think and speak about him."

J.I. Packer

God Is Triune

THE BIG IDEA

There is one God, but in the unity of the one God are three coequal and coeternal persons—the Father, the Son, and the Holy Spirit—who are equal in deity but distinct in personhood.

What You Need to Know

▶ There is only one true God (Isaiah 44:6-8).

▶ And yet there are three persons called God: the Father (1 Peter 1:2), Jesus the Son (Hebrews 1:8), and the Holy Spirit (Acts 5:3-4).

▶ There is three-in-oneness within the one God (Matthew 28:19; 2 Corinthians 13:14). That is, there are three "whos" (persons) in one "what" (God).

Verses to Contemplate

One God. "Thus says the LORD...I am the first and I am the last; besides me there is no god" (Isaiah 44:6).

Three Persons. "Go therefore and make disciples of all

nations, baptizing them in the name of the Father and of the Son and of the Holy Spirit" (Matthew 28:19).

Truths That Transform

Each of the three persons of the Trinity played a pivotal role in your salvation.

1. The Father sovereignly elected you to salvation (1 Peter 1:2).
2. The Son redeemed you at the cross (2 Corinthians 5:21).
3. The Holy Spirit regenerated you at the moment of conversion (John 3:5-7).

A Quote to Ponder

"If there be one God subsisting in three persons, then let us give equal reverence to all the persons in the Trinity."

Thomas Watson

God the Father

THE BIG IDEA

God the Father is the personal, sovereign, and majestic Creator of the universe, who reigns from on high.

What You Need to Know

- ▶ The Father is the First Person of the Trinity (Matthew 28:19; 2 Corinthians 13:14).

- ▶ God the Father (1 Peter 1:2) is everywhere-present (Psalm 139:7-10), all-knowing (Romans 11:33), and all-powerful (1 Peter 1:5).

- ▶ The Father planned and ordained salvation (Isaiah 53:6,10; John 3:16) and elected certain ones to salvation (Romans 8:29-30; Ephesians 1:4). He is sovereign over all things (Isaiah 46:10).

Verses to Contemplate

There is "one God and Father of all, who is over all and through all and in all" (Ephesians 4:6).

"See what kind of love the Father has given to us, that we should be called children of God" (1 John 3:1).

The false gods of paganism cannot compare with God the Father. This was taught in the Old Testament through...

Affirmation. "You alone are God" (Psalm 86:10).

Negation. "There is none like God" (Deuteronomy 33:26).

Rhetorical questions. "Who is like you, O LORD, among the gods?" (Exodus 15:11).

Truths That Transform

1. The Father's love for you is infinite (1 John 3:1).
2. The Father's mercy toward you is immeasurable (2 Corinthians 1:3).
3. The Father brings comfort (2 Corinthians 1:3).
4. We can cry out to God, "Abba! Father!" (Galatians 4:6).

A Quote to Ponder

"[The Father's plan of salvation] includes the means by which salvation is to be provided, the objectives that are to be realized, the persons that are to benefit by it, the conditions on which it is to be available, and the agents and means by which it is to be applied."

Henry C. Thiessen

God the Son

THE BIG IDEA

Jesus Christ—the second person of the Trinity—is the divine and eternal Son of God, the Savior and Redeemer of humankind.

What You Need to Know

▶ Jesus is the second person of the Trinity (Matthew 28:19; 2 Corinthians 13:14).

▶ "Jesus" means "the Lord saves" (Matthew 1:21).

▶ "Christ" and "Messiah" both mean "anointed one" (John 1:41).

▶ Jesus is God (Hebrews 1:8) and Lord (Matthew 22:43-44).

▶ In the incarnation, Jesus was 100 percent God (Colossians 2:9) and 100 percent man (Galatians 4:4-5; Hebrews 2:14).

▶ Jesus came to earth as the Savior (John 4:42) and Redeemer (1 Peter 1:18-19).

Verses to Contemplate

"He will be great and will be called the Son of the Most High" (Luke 1:32).

"He was even calling God his own Father, making himself equal with God" (John 5:18).

FAST FACTS
Divine Names and Titles of Christ

Yahweh—the self-existent one (John 8:58)

Elohim—Mighty God (Isaiah 9:6)

Lord—the sovereign ruler (Romans 10:12)

Truths That Transform

1. Jesus's teachings are final (Matthew 24:35).
2. He unflinchingly placed His teachings above those of Moses and the prophets—and in a Jewish culture at that (Matthew 5:21-22).
3. He always spoke in His own authority: "Truly, truly, I say to you…" (John 5:24).
4. He asserted, "Heaven and earth will pass away, but my words will not pass away" (Mark 13:31).

A Quote to Ponder

"Christianity is not devotion to work, or to a cause, or a doctrine, but devotion to a person, the Lord Jesus Christ."

Oswald Chambers

6

God the Holy Spirit

THE BIG IDEA

The Holy Spirit—the third person of the Trinity—plays a crucial role in the salvation and sanctification of every Christian.

What You Need to Know

▶ The Holy Spirit is the third person of the Trinity (Matthew 28:19; 2 Corinthians 13:14).

▶ The Holy Spirit is God (Acts 5:3-4) and has divine attributes (for example, Romans 15:19).

▶ The Holy Spirit is a person with a mind (Romans 8:27), emotions (Ephesians 4:30), and a will (1 Corinthians 12:11).

▶ He teaches (John 14:26), guides (Romans 8:14), restrains sin (Genesis 6:3), and much more.

Verses to Contemplate

"The Helper, the Holy Spirit, whom the Father will send in my name, he will teach you all things and bring to your remembrance all that I have said to you" (John 14:26).

"You will receive power when the Holy Spirit has come upon you, and you will be my witnesses in Jerusalem and in all Judea and Samaria, and to the end of the earth" (Acts 1:8).

FAST FACTS
Evidence for the Holy Spirit's Personhood

The Holy Spirit teaches (John 14:26).

The Holy Spirit testifies (John 15:26).

The Holy Spirit issues commands (Acts 8:29).

The Holy Spirit prays (Romans 8:26).

Truths That Transform

We are wisest to perpetually walk in dependence on the Holy Spirit (Galatians 5:16) because He...

1. gives us spiritual gifts (1 Corinthians 12)
2. comforts us (John 16:7)
3. glorifies Jesus (John 15:26)
4. guides us (John 14:25-26)
5. convicts us of sin (John 16:7-14)
6. produces fruit in us (Galatians 5:22-26)

A Quote to Ponder

"Though every believer has the Holy Spirit, the Holy Spirit does not have every believer."

A.W. Tozer

The Living God

THE BIG IDEA

Our God is a *living* God who personally interacts with His people.

What You Need to Know

- ▶ We are not to trust in the dead idols of paganism but in the one true living God, who is the Creator of the universe (Acts 14:15).

- ▶ The living God is among His people (Joshua 3:10), and He communicates with them (Deuteronomy 5:26).

- ▶ A relationship with the living God brings joy (Psalm 84:2). Believers perpetually yearn for fellowship with Him (Psalm 42:2).

- ▶ Believers place their hope in the living God, who saves His people (1 Timothy 4:10).

Verses to Contemplate

"We bring you good news, that you should turn from these vain things to a living God, who made the heaven and the earth and the sea and all that is in them" (Acts 14:15).

"As a deer pants for flowing streams, so pants my soul for you, O God" (Psalm 42:1).

Truths That Transform

1. Sin and unbelief can cause one to fall away from the living God (Hebrews 3:12).
2. Trusting in the living God brings miraculous results (1 Samuel 17:26-36). Remember this the next time you need a miracle.
3. The living God providentially protects His followers (Daniel 6:20). This should give you a sense of security in daily life.

A Quote to Ponder

"Watch the hand of this living God intervening, in answer to His people's prayers, working miracles, converting thousands, opening prison doors, and raising the dead, guiding His messengers to people and places they had never thought of, supervising the whole operation and every figure in it so as to work out His purpose in the end."

R.T. France

God Is a Spirit

THE BIG IDEA

God is a spirit—nonphysical and invisible.

What You Need to Know

- ▶ God is spirit (John 4:24).
- ▶ A spirit does not have flesh and bones (Luke 24:39).
- ▶ Because God is a spirit, He is invisible (1 Timothy 1:17; Colossians 1:15).
- ▶ When Jesus became a man in the incarnation (Galatians 4:4), He was a physical manifestation of the invisible God (John 1:14,18).

Verses to Contemplate

"God is spirit" (John 4:24).

"To the King of the ages, immortal, invisible, the only God, be honor and glory" (1 Timothy 1:17).

"The LORD spoke to you out of the midst of the fire. You heard the sound of words, but saw no form; there was only a voice" (Deuteronomy 4:12).

Truths That Transform

1. We do not outwardly perceive God's presence, but He is nevertheless always with us.

2. There is nowhere we can go where He is not there with us.

3. The psalmist mused, "Where shall I go from your Spirit? Or where shall I flee from your presence?" (Psalm 139:7).

4. Take comfort in the reality that God's invisible presence is with you at all times and in all places, regardless of your circumstances.

A Quote to Ponder

"Because God is a spirit, it follows that He is immaterial and invisible. Everything about God is marvelous and mysterious to us."

John Phillips

God Is Personal and Relational

THE BIG IDEA

God is a personal being who engages in intimate personal relationships with His people.

What You Need to Know

- ▶ Adam and Eve enjoyed direct, intimate fellowship with God. The Lord came into the Garden of Eden to visit with them (Genesis 3:8).

- ▶ Others also came to know God personally. "Enoch walked with God" (Genesis 5:24). "Noah walked with God" (Genesis 6:9). "The LORD used to speak to Moses face to face, as a man speaks to his friend" (Exodus 33:11).

Verses to Contemplate

"Thus says the LORD...'Let him who boasts boast in this, that he understands and knows me'" (Jeremiah 9:23-24).

"This is eternal life, that they know you the only true God, and Jesus Christ whom you have sent" (John 17:3).

A person engages in active relationships with others. God does this with us!

Believers can call God "Abba" (Romans 8:15), a term meaning "papa" or "daddy."

Paul spoke of God as a personal "Father of mercies" (2 Corinthians 1:3).

Truths That Transform

1. God declared Adam's loneliness to be "not good" (Genesis 2:18). God made man as a social being (Genesis 2:21-23).

2. The most important relationship man was created to enter into is with God Himself (Jeremiah 9:23-24).

3. The more time we spend with God, the more intimately we come to know Him.

A Quote to Ponder

"What were we made for? To know God! What aim should we set ourselves in life? To know God!...What is the best thing in life, bringing more joy, delight, and contentment, than anything else? Knowledge of God."

J.I. Packer

God Is with Us

THE BIG IDEA

God is actively present within the creation and in human history. Theologians refer to this as God's *immanence*.

What You Need to Know

▶ God is immanent—He is actively present within the creation, in human history, and in the direct presence of human beings (Psalm 139:8).

▶ This does not contradict the truth that God is also transcendent—that is, He is separate from and high above the creation (1 Kings 8:27).

▶ God is in heaven but is also on the earth below. "Can a man hide himself in secret places so that I cannot see him? declares the LORD. Do I not fill heaven and earth? declares the LORD" (Jeremiah 23:24).

Verses to Contemplate

"The LORD is God in heaven above and on the earth beneath" (Deuteronomy 4:39).

"He is actually not far from each one of us" (Acts 17:27).

"If I ascend to heaven, you are there! If I make my bed in Sheol, you are there!" (Psalm 139:8)

Truths That Transform

1. Knowing that God is immanent comforts us, for He is always near, regardless of where we go (Psalm 139:7-10).

2. He is near in our times of loneliness, need, and illness. He is near when we feel threatened.

3. Let the truth of God's immanence be a source of perpetual comfort to you.

A Quote to Ponder

The Christian finds safety not in the absence of danger but in the presence of God.

Anonymous

God Is High Above Us

THE BIG IDEA

God is other than, separate from, and independent from the created universe, including humanity. Theologians refer to this as God's *transcendence*.

What You Need to Know

- ▶ God is other than and separate from the created universe and from humanity (Psalm 113:5-6).
- ▶ God is "high and lifted up" (Isaiah 57:15).
- ▶ God is also immanent. He is active within creation and among humans (Acts 17:27).

Verses to Contemplate

"Behold, heaven and the highest heaven cannot contain you; how much less this house that I have built!" (1 Kings 8:27).

"Who is like the LORD our God, who is seated on high, who looks far down on the heavens and the earth?" (Psalm 113:5-6).

"He is highly exalted" (Psalm 47:9).

"You, O LORD, are most high over all the earth; you are exalted far above all gods" (Psalm 97:9).

"His name alone is exalted" (Psalm 148:13).

Truths That Transform

1. "My thoughts are not your thoughts, neither are your ways my ways, declares the LORD. For as the heavens are higher than the earth, so are my ways higher than your ways and my thoughts than your thoughts" (Isaiah 55:8-9).

2. Don't put God in a box. He can act in ways you can't even begin to fathom.

3. Because God's thoughts are far above our own limited thoughts, we should trust Him with our trials and difficulties.

4. He is aware of far more creative solutions than we could ever conceive of.

A Quote to Ponder

"The world appears very little to a soul that contemplates the greatness of God."

Brother Lawrence

God Has Many Names

THE BIG IDEA

We learn a great deal about God from the descriptive names ascribed to Him in the Bible.

What You Need to Know

In the ancient world, a name was not a mere label as it is today. It revealed characteristics about the person. God's names reveal a lot about Him:

- ▶ God's name *Yahweh* points to His self-existence for all eternity (Exodus 3:14-15).
- ▶ God's name *Elohim* means "Strong One" (Isaiah 54:5; Jeremiah 32:27).
- ▶ God's name *Yahweh-Nissi* means "the Lord Our Banner" (Exodus 17:15).

Verses to Contemplate

"Behold, I am the LORD [*Yahweh*], the God [*Elohim*] of all flesh. Is anything too hard for me?" (Jeremiah 32:27).

"The LORD of hosts [*Yahweh Sabaoth*] has sworn: As I

have planned, so shall it be, and as I have purposed, so shall it stand" (Isaiah 14:24).

Truths That Transform

1. As *Yahweh Sabaoth*, God commands the angelic army that watches over us and protects us (Psalm 91:11).
2. As *Elohim*, God acts mightily on our behalf (Jeremiah 32:27).
3. As *El Shaddai*, God nourishes us in compassion, grace, and mercy (Genesis 49:25).
4. As *Yahweh-Nissi*, God gives us victory in the trials we face (Exodus 17:15).
5. The God of many names is on your side!

A Quote to Ponder

*"Where the name of God is not known,
he himself cannot be known."*

John Gill

God Is Self-Existent

THE BIG IDEA

God has life in Himself and does not depend on anyone or anything outside Himself for His existence.

What You Need to Know

- ▶ God is not a contingent being. He is eternally self-existent. He does not derive from or depend on anyone or anything for His existence.

- ▶ God is the uncaused First Cause who brought all other things into being (Genesis 1; John 1:3).

- ▶ God has the ground of His existence in Himself. He is utterly independent in His being (John 5:26).

- ▶ God's name *Yahweh* describes Him as eternally self-existent (see Exodus 3:14-15). He never came into being at a point in time. He is literally the Eternal One.

Verses to Contemplate

"The Father has life in himself" (John 5:26).

"Before the mountains were brought forth, or ever you

had formed the earth and the world, from everlasting to everlasting you are God" (Psalm 90:2).

Truths That Transform

1. Like God the Father, Jesus has life in Himself (John 5:26). "In him was life" (John 1:4).

2. Jesus is "the way, and the truth, and the life" (John 14:6).

3. Jesus is "the resurrection and the life" (John 11:25).

4. You and I do not have life in ourselves. We are destined to experience death. But in Jesus Christ, the One who has life in Himself, we have eternal life.

5. Rejoice that you have eternal life in Jesus!

A Quote to Ponder

"God's eternity and self-existence are interrelated concepts... If God exists endlessly, then He never came into existence nor was He ever caused to come into existence. He is endlessly self-existent."

Charles Ryrie

God Is Eternal

THE BIG IDEA

God is an eternal being—there was never a time in which He did not exist.

What You Need to Know

▶ God transcends all temporal limitations.

▶ God is the King of the ages (1 Timothy 1:17), who alone is immortal (6:16).

▶ He is "the Alpha and the Omega" (Revelation 1:8) and "the first and...the last" (Isaiah 44:6; 48:12).

▶ He exists "from eternity" (Isaiah 43:13 NASB) and "from everlasting to everlasting" (Psalms 41:13; 90:2).

▶ He lives forever from eternal ages past (Psalm 102:12,27; Isaiah 57:15).

Verses to Contemplate

God "alone has immortality" (1 Timothy 6:16).

The Lord God said, "I am the first and I am the last; besides me there is no god" (Isaiah 44:6).

God is "the One who is high and lifted up, who inhabits eternity" (Isaiah 57:15).

God is "the King of ages, immortal" (1 Timothy 1:17).

Truths That Transform

1. Human leaders, countries, and even family members come and go.
2. A comforting ramification of God's eternal nature is that He will never cease to exist. He will always be there for us (Psalm 46:1-3).
3. God's continued providential oversight of our lives is thereby assured (see Psalm 23).
4. His gift of eternal life to us is also assured (John 3:16).

A Quote to Ponder

"[God is] the eternal without beginning, He who is above the whole course of time, He who in harmony beyond explanation possesses unity and life, the Father, the Son, and the Holy Spirit, the basis of eternity, the Living One, the only God."

Erich Sauer

God Is Everywhere-Present

THE BIG IDEA

God is everywhere-present. Theologians refer to this as God's *omnipresence*.

What You Need to Know

- ▶ God is omnipresent. "Omni" means all. God is all-present, or everywhere-present.
- ▶ This means there is nowhere one can go where God is not (Psalm 139:7-8; Jeremiah 23:23-24; Acts 17:27-28).
- ▶ Nevertheless, God is distinct from creation and from humankind (Numbers 23:19; Ecclesiastes 5:2; Hebrews 11:3).

Verses to Contemplate

"Where shall I go from your Spirit? Or where shall I flee from your presence? If I ascend to heaven, you are there! If I make my bed in Sheol, you are there!" (Psalm 139:7-8).

"He is actually not far from each one of us, for 'In him we live and move and have our being'" (Acts 17:27-28).

Pantheism, which says all is God, destroys distinctions between the Creator and the creation.

If all is God, we have no explanation for evil.

It violates common sense, doing away with the distinction between myself and anything else.

Truths That Transform

1. Because God is omnipresent, He is with you even in the worst moments of your life.
2. Psalm 46:1 says, "God is our refuge and strength, a very present help in trouble."
3. This means God is present with you to help you in the midst of pain, sickness, sorrow, anger, grief, bitterness, betrayal, abuse, warfare, natural disasters, accidents, and personal loss.
4. God is present with us 24/7. There's never a time when we do not have His full attention.

A Quote to Ponder

"We may ignore, but we can nowhere evade, the presence of God. The world is crowded with Him. He walks everywhere incognito."

C.S. Lewis

God Is All-Powerful

THE BIG IDEA

God is all-powerful. Theologians refer to this as God's *omnipotence*.

What You Need to Know

- God is omnipotent. "Omni" means "all." God is all-powerful.

- Scripture repeatedly declares that God is almighty (Revelation 19:6).

- God's power is abundant (Psalm 147:5) and incomparably great (2 Chronicles 20:6; Ephesians 1:19-21).

- No one can reverse God (Isaiah 43:13).

- Nothing is impossible with God (Matthew 19:26) and nothing is too difficult for Him (Genesis 18:14; Jeremiah 32:17,27).

Verses to Contemplate

"Ah, Lord GOD! It is you who have made the heavens and the earth by your great power and by your outstretched arm! Nothing is too hard for you" (Jeremiah 32:17).

"In your hand are power and might, so that none is able to withstand you" (2 Chronicles 20:6).

Truths That Transform

1. Because God is all-powerful, He is able to fulfill all His promises in Scripture (Joshua 21:45).
2. God has the power to see believers securely into heaven without any falling away (John 6:39).
3. The same awesome power that raised Jesus from the dead will one day raise us from the dead (1 Corinthians 15:51-55).
4. Rest in the knowledge that all is in the hands of our all-powerful God (Isaiah 14:27; 43:13).
5. God's power is made perfect in weakness (2 Corinthians 12:9).

A Quote to Ponder

"Difficulties provide a platform on which the Lord can display His power."

J. Hudson Taylor

17

God Is All-Knowing

THE BIG IDEA

God is all-knowing. Theologians refer to this as God's *omniscience*.

What You Need to Know

- ▶ God is omniscient. "Omni" means "all." God is all-knowing.

- ▶ God knows all things—actual and possible (Matthew 11:21-23), past (Isaiah 41:22), present (Hebrews 4:13), and future (Isaiah 46:10).

- ▶ God is outside of time. His knowledge is from the vantage point of eternity. The past, present, and future are simultaneously present to Him.

- ▶ Because He knows all things, His knowledge cannot increase or decrease.

- ▶ Psalm 147:5 affirms that God's understanding has no limit. His knowledge is infinite (Psalms 33:13-15; 139:11-12; 147:5).

Verses to Contemplate

"He knows everything" (1 John 3:20).

"His understanding is beyond measure" (Psalm 147:5).

Truths That Transform

1. One of the great things about God's omniscience is that nothing in our lives will cause Him to change His mind about including us in His family (Psalm 139:1-4).

2. When we become Christians, God is fully aware of every sin we have ever committed and ever will commit (Psalm 147:5).

3. God knows everything about us and accepts us anyway, so every child of God can have a profound sense of security in salvation (see Hebrews 13:5).

A Quote to Ponder

"Because God knows all things perfectly, he knows no thing better than any other thing, but all things equally well. He never discovers anything, he is never surprised, never amazed."

A.W. Tozer

God Is Sovereign

THE BIG IDEA

God is absolutely sovereign. He has supreme power and authority over all things in the universe.

What You Need to Know

- ▶ God rules the universe, controls all things, and is Lord over all (Ephesians 1).
- ▶ All things are within the scope of His absolute dominion (Psalm 93:1).
- ▶ Despite the plans humans may make, God is absolutely sovereign over each of them and their circumstances (Proverbs 16:9; 19:21).
- ▶ God does all He pleases to do (Isaiah 46:10) and purposes to do (Isaiah 14:24).

Verses to Contemplate

"I am God, and there is no other; I am God, and there is none like me…'My counsel shall stand, and I will accomplish all my purpose'" (Isaiah 46:9-10).

"The LORD of hosts has sworn: 'As I have planned, so

shall it be, and as I have purposed, so shall it stand'" (Isaiah 14:24).

Truths That Transform

1. Regardless of what we encounter, the knowledge that our sovereign God is in control is like a firm anchor in the midst of life's storms (Isaiah 14:24; 46:10).

2. In Romans 8:28 the apostle Paul explains, "We know that for those who love God all things work together for good, for those who are called according to his purpose."

3. We should therefore daily rest in God's sovereign oversight of all our circumstances— especially when life throws us a punch.

A Quote to Ponder

"As children of a sovereign God, we are never victims of our circumstances."

Charles Stanley

God Is a Planner

THE BIG IDEA

The decrees of God are the eternal plans He made before the creation of the universe.

What You Need to Know

- ▶ God rules the universe (Ephesians 1), reigns with absolute dominion (Psalm 93:1), and does all that He purposes to do (Isaiah 14:24).

- ▶ God formulated a "definite plan" in eternity past (Acts 2:23) that includes all things (Ephesians 1:11).

- ▶ God's ongoing providential actions in the world are the outworking of His eternal decrees (Acts 4:28).

Verses to Contemplate

"Jesus [was delivered up] according to the definite plan and foreknowledge of God" (Acts 2:23).

"The Gentiles and the peoples of Israel [gathered together to do] whatever your hand and your plan had predestined to take place" (Acts 4:27-28).

Truths That Transform

1. According to God's sovereign plan, you and I are responsible for our freewill choices and will be held accountable for them.

2. God decreed that if we choose righteous living, things will go well for us. However, He also decreed that if we choose unrighteous living, things will go badly for us (Psalm 1).

3. God also decreed to do some things only in answer to prayer. "You do not have, because you do not ask" (James 4:2).

A Quote to Ponder

"The decrees of God are his eternal purpose, according to the counsel of his will, whereby, for his own glory, he hath foreordained whatsoever comes to pass."

The Westminster Shorter Catechism

20

God Is Holy

THE BIG IDEA

Our God is a holy God, which means He is wholly set apart from sin and wholly set apart unto perfect righteousness.

What You Need to Know

▶ The word "holy" means "set apart."

▶ Because God is holy, He is not only entirely separate (or "set apart") from all evil, but He is also absolutely righteous (Leviticus 19:2).

▶ He is pure in every way. "God is light, and in him is no darkness at all" (1 John 1:5).

▶ Heavenly beings proclaim that God is "holy, holy, holy" (Isaiah 6:3). The repetition of the word emphasizes God's absolute holiness.

Verses to Contemplate

"Who is like you, majestic in holiness?" (Exodus 15:11).

"There is none holy like the LORD" (1 Samuel 2:2).

"Holy and awesome is his name!" (Psalm 111:9).

"Holy, holy, holy is the LORD of hosts; the whole earth is full of his glory!" (Isaiah 6:3).

Truths That Transform

1. Because God is holy, if we are to fellowship with Him, we must take our personal holiness seriously (1 John 1:5-9).

2. Scripture instructs, "You shall be holy, for I am holy" (1 Peter 1:16; see also Leviticus 11:44).

3. This means that you and I are to be set apart from sinful behavior and set apart unto righteous living.

4. Scripture instructs us, "Present your bodies as a living sacrifice, holy and acceptable to God, which is your spiritual worship" (Romans 12:1).

A Quote to Ponder

"When we understand the character of God, when we grasp something of His holiness, then we begin to understand the radical character of our sin."

R.C. Sproul

21

God Is True

THE BIG IDEA

God is by nature true and communicates only truth.

What You Need to Know

- ▶ God is true in the sense that He is fully consistent with Himself, He has revealed Himself to others as He really is, and His revelation is true and reliable.

- ▶ The God of the Bible is the only true God (John 17:3). There is no other.

- ▶ The true God communicates only truth (John 17:17). Everything He says is utterly trustworthy.

Verses to Contemplate

"We know that the Son of God has come and has given us understanding, so that we may know him who is true; and we are in him who is true, in his Son Jesus Christ. He is the true God and eternal life" (1 John 5:20).

"God is not man, that he should lie, or a son of man, that he should change his mind. Has he said, and will he not do it?" (Numbers 23:19)

Hold on to truth (Proverbs 23:23).

Speak the truth (Zechariah 8:16).

Worship God in truth (John 4:23-24).

Live by the truth (John 3:21).

Truths That Transform

You can trust your Bible.

▶ "Your word is truth" (John 17:17).

▶ "The word of the LORD is upright" (Psalm 33:4).

▶ "All your commandments are true" (Psalm 119:151).

Rejoice that you worship the true God, who is also the Revealer of truth!

A Quote to Ponder

*"God the Father, God the Son, God the Holy Spirit—
three Persons, one God. This is the true God,
the real God. The gods of the pagans do not
faintly resemble Him, nor are the gods of the
world's false religions remotely like Him."*

John Phillips

22

God Is Righteous and Just

THE BIG IDEA

God is wholly and perfectly righteous and just.

What You Need to Know

- ▶ God is intrinsically righteous (Deuteronomy 32:4; Psalm 19:9; 145:17; Acts 17:31).

- ▶ The Hebrew and Greek words for righteousness contain the idea of conformity to a standard. All God's actions conform to His own perfect standard.

- ▶ God is also just. He is never partial or unfair in His dealings (Genesis 18:25; Psalm 11:7; Romans 3:26).

Verses to Contemplate

"The LORD is righteous; he loves righteous deeds" (Psalm 11:7).

"Righteousness and justice are the foundation of your throne" (Psalm 89:14).

"He will judge the world with righteousness, and the peoples with equity" (Psalm 98:9).

He calls His children to be righteous (Matthew 6:33).

He calls His children to be just (Micah 6:8).

Truths That Transform

1. The fact that God is righteous and just is a comfort for those who have been wronged in life. They can rest assured that God will right all wrongs in the end.

2. It is a warning for those who think they have been getting away with evil. Justice will prevail in the end! All people— Christians and unbelievers —will have to give an account of their actions before God (2 Corinthians 5:10; Revelation 20:11-15).

A Quote to Ponder

"God's righteousness (or justice) is the natural expression of His holiness. If He is infinitely pure, then He must be opposed to all sin, and that opposition to sin must be demonstrated in His treatment of His creatures. When we read that God is righteous or just, we are being assured that His actions toward us are in perfect agreement with His holy nature."

Richard Strauss

23

God Is Loving and Gracious

THE BIG IDEA

God is, by nature, love. His grace is limitless.

What You Need to Know

▸ God isn't just characterized by love; He is the personification of love (1 John 4:8).

▸ God's love does not depend on the lovability of the object (human beings). God loves us despite the fact that we are fallen in sin (John 3:16). (God loves the sinner even though He hates the sin.)

▸ God is also full of grace toward us (Exodus 34:6). "Grace" means "unmerited favor" (see Ephesians 2:4-9).

Verses to Contemplate

"God is love" (1 John 4:8).

"You, O Lord, are a God merciful and gracious, slow to anger and abounding in steadfast love and faithfulness" (Psalm 86:15).

"You are a God ready to forgive, gracious and merciful, slow to anger and abounding in steadfast love" (Nehemiah 9:17).

FAST FACTS
God's Grace Through Jesus Christ

Grace is a gift of Christ (Ephesians 4:7).

Grace through Christ strengthens us (2 Timothy 2:1).

Grace in Christ is immeasurable (Ephesians 2:7).

Grace in Christ can overflow (1 Timothy 1:14).

Grace in Christ can be lavished upon us (2 Peter 1:2).

Truths That Transform

1. God is loving and gracious, so you and I should be loving and gracious toward others.
2. "Anyone who does not love does not know God, because God is love" (1 John 4:8).
3. "Aim for restoration, comfort one another, agree with one another, live in peace; and the God of love and peace will be with you" (2 Corinthians 13:11).

A Quote to Ponder

"Abounding sin is the terror of the world, but abounding grace is the hope of mankind."

A.W. Tozer

24

God Is Merciful

THE BIG IDEA

God is merciful in withholding punishment when He can—especially among the repentant. Those who reject God's mercy and continue to sin receive God's wrath.

What You Need to Know

- ▶ To say that God is merciful is to say that He withholds the punishment we deserve.
- ▶ God delights in showing mercy. In His mercy, God is slow to anger (Exodus 34:6).
- ▶ God loves that which conforms to His character, but He hates that which violates His character.
- ▶ God's wrath is therefore justly directed against those who sin and do not repent (Romans 1:18).

Verses to Contemplate

"His mercies never come to an end; they are new every morning" (Lamentations 3:22-23).

"The LORD, the LORD, a God merciful and gracious" (Exodus 34:6).

"The wrath of God is revealed from heaven against all ungodliness and unrighteousness of men" (Romans 1:18).

Truths That Transform

1. Jesus Christ makes God's mercy available to us (Hebrews 2:17).
2. "Let us then with confidence draw near to the throne of grace, that we may receive mercy and find grace to help in time of need" (Hebrews 4:16).
3. As the "Father of mercies," God is the ultimate source of comfort for the afflicted (2 Corinthians 1:3).

A Quote to Ponder

"As God's mercies are new every morning toward his people, so his anger is new every morning against the wicked."

Matthew Henry

25

God Is Unchanging

THE BIG IDEA

God is unchanging in His being, perfection, purposes, and promises. Theologians refer to this as God's *immutability*.

What You Need to Know

- To say that God is immutable is to say that His nature will never change.

- He will always be holy (Isaiah 6:3), righteous (Deuteronomy 32:4), merciful (Lamentations 3:22-23), all-knowing (Isaiah 40:13-14), all-powerful (Genesis 18:14), and everywhere-present (Psalm 139:7-12).

- God is also unchanging in His sovereign purposes (Isaiah 46:10) and His promises (Numbers 23:19; see also 1 Samuel 15:29).

Verses to Contemplate

"For I the LORD do not change" (Malachi 3:6).

"With [the Father of lights] there is no variation or shadow due to change" (James 1:17).

"God desired to show...the unchangeable character of his purpose" (Hebrews 6:17).

FAST FACTS
Implications of God's Immutability

God's Word is just as reliable today as it was in biblical days.

The conditions of fellowship with God remain the same—we must avoid sin.

We can live by faith. God, the object of our faith, is always reliable—there are no exceptions.

Truths That Transform

Because God is immutable...

1. He will never change the terms of our salvation (Galatians 1:8).
2. He will always fulfill His promises (Joshua 21:45).
3. He will never change His mind about human sin or compromise in the slightest degree with it (1 Peter 1:16).

A Quote to Ponder

"Immutability reminds us that God's attitudes toward sin do not change. Therefore, God can never be coaxed or compromised into changing."

Charles Ryrie

26

God Is Glorious

THE BIG IDEA

God is a being of ineffable and resplendent glory.

What You Need to Know

- ▶ Brilliant light consistently accompanies the divine manifestation of His glory (Matthew 17:2-3; 1 Timothy 6:16; Revelation 1:16).

- ▶ From the throne of God in heaven come relentless flashes of lightning (Revelation 4:5), pointing to His awesome glory.

- ▶ At the second coming, Jesus will appear in resplendent glory (Mark 13:26).

- ▶ The future eternal city, the New Jerusalem, will be illuminated by God's glory (Revelation 21:11; 22:5).

Verses to Contemplate

"The appearance of the glory of the LORD was like a devouring fire on the top of the mountain in the sight of the people of Israel" (Exodus 24:17).

"The glory of the LORD filled the tabernacle" (Exodus 40:34).

Truths That Transform

1. When the God of glory appeared to people in Bible times, they fell to their knees (Revelation 1:17).
2. "This perishable body must put on the imperishable, and this mortal body must put on immortality" (1 Corinthians 15:53).
3. In our upgraded resurrected bodies, we will dwell with God face-to-face (Revelation 21:3).

A Quote to Ponder

"The light in which He dwells is superior to all things visible; it is something other than the radiance of all suns and stars. It is not to be beheld by earthly eyes; it is 'unapproachable' (1 Tim. 6:16), far removed from all things this side (2 Cor. 12:4)."

Erich Sauer

27

The Worship of God

THE BIG IDEA

The proper response of the creature to the Creator is to worship Him for all eternity.

What You Need to Know

- ▶ God alone is to be worshipped (Matthew 4:10; Acts 14:11-18; Revelation 19:10).
- ▶ Worship involves reverencing God, adoring Him, praising Him, venerating Him, and paying homage to Him (1 Samuel 15:22-23; Isaiah 29:13).
- ▶ Worship is the proper response of a creature to the divine Creator (see Psalm 95:6).
- ▶ Worship can be congregational (1 Corinthians 11–14) or individual (see Romans 12:1).

Verses to Contemplate

"You shall worship no other god, for the LORD, whose name is Jealous, is a jealous God" (Exodus 34:14).

"Oh come, let us worship and bow down; let us kneel before the LORD, our Maker!" (Psalm 95:6).

"Ascribe to the LORD the glory due his name; worship the LORD in the splendor of holiness" (Psalm 29:2).

FAST FACTS
Christ, as God, Was Worshipped By...

Thomas (John 20:28)	a ruler (Matthew 9:18)
angels (Hebrews 1:6)	a blind man (John 9:38)
wise men (Matthew 2:11)	a woman (Matthew 15:25)
a leper (Matthew 8:2)	His disciples (Matthew 28:17)

Truths That Transform

1. The most common way of worshipping God is with songs, hymns, and rituals, wherein we express adoration and praise to Him.
2. Scripture also teaches that we can worship God by daily giving ourselves completely to Him.
3. "I appeal to you therefore, brothers, by the mercies of God, to present your bodies as a living sacrifice, holy and acceptable to God, which is your spiritual worship" (Romans 12:1).

A Quote to Ponder

"The most valuable thing the Psalms do for me is to express the same delight in God which made David dance."

C.S. Lewis

28

Face-to-Face with God

THE BIG IDEA

In heaven we will dwell in God's direct presence, face-to-face, and know Him with unhindered intimacy.

What You Need to Know

- ▶ In heaven, we will finally have unhindered, full access to God (Psalm 17:15; Revelation 22:4).

- ▶ There can be no greater joy than to see God's face and fellowship with Him forever (John 14:3; 2 Corinthians 5:6-8; Philippians 1:23).

- ▶ God, "who dwells in unapproachable light" (1 Timothy 6:16), will dwell among His people.

Verses to Contemplate

"They will see his face" (Revelation 22:4).

"As for me, I shall behold your face" (Psalm 17:15).

"Behold, the dwelling place of God is with man. He will dwell with them, and they will be his people, and God himself will be with them as their God" (Revelation 21:3).

In heaven our fellowship with God will be unhindered by...

sin (Revelation 21:27)

unrepentant sinners (Revelation 20:11-15)

Satan (Revelation 20:10)

Truths That Transform

1. Once we are in heaven, our fellowship with God will no longer be interrupted by sin and defeat.
2. Our fellowship with God will be continuous and unbroken, for sin will no longer be among us.
3. To fellowship with God will be the essence of heavenly life, the fount and source of all blessing (Revelation 21:1-5).
4. The crowning wonder of our experience in the eternal city will be the perpetual and endless exploration of that unutterable beauty, majesty, love, holiness, and grace which is God Himself.

A Quote to Ponder

"[In heaven, we will have] an undiminished, unwearied sight of His infinite glory and beauty, bringing us infinite and eternal delight."

John MacArthur

God and His Promises

THE BIG IDEA

Our wondrous God has made many blessed promises in His Word, and He makes good on all of them!

What You Need to Know

- ▶ God keeps all His promises (see Numbers 23:19; Joshua 23:14; 1 Kings 8:56).

- ▶ Therefore every Christian can benefit by studying these promises and acting on them daily.

Verses to Contemplate

"You know in your hearts and souls, all of you, that not one word has failed of all the good things that the LORD your God promised concerning you. All have come to pass for you; not one of them has failed" (Joshua 23:14).

"God is not man, that he should lie, or a son of man, that he should change his mind. Has he said, and will he not do it? Or has he spoken, and will he not fulfill it?" (Numbers 23:19).

A Quote to Ponder

"God's promises are like the stars—the darker the night, the brighter they shine!"

David Nicholas

Bibliography

Boice, James M. *The Sovereign God.* Downers Grove, IL: InterVarsity, 1978.

Charnock, Stephen. *The Existence and Attributes of God.* Grand Rapids, MI: Baker, 1996.

Craig, William Lane. *The Existence of God and the Beginning of the Universe.* San Bernardino, CA: Here's Life, 1979.

Davis, Jimmy H. and Harry L. Poe. *Designer Universe.* Nashville, TN: Broadman & Holman, 2002.

Dembski, William A. *Intelligent Design.* Downers Grove, IL: InterVarsity, 1999.

France, R.T. *The Living God.* Downers Grove, IL: Inter Varsity, 1972.

Geisler, Norman and Frank Turek. *I Don't Have Enough Faith to Be an Atheist.* Wheaton, IL: Crossway, 2004.

Lightner, Robert P. *The God of the Bible.* Grand Rapids, MI: Baker, 1978.

Moreland, J.P. and Kai Nielsen. *Does God Exist? The Great Debate.* Nashville, TN: Nelson, 1990.

Packer, J.I. *Knowing God.* Downers Grove, IL: InterVarsity, 1979.

Pink, A.W. *The Attributes of God.* Alexandria, LA: Lamplighter, n.d.

Pink, A.W. *The Sovereignty of God.* London, England: The Banner of Truth Trust, 1972.

Tozer, A.W. *The Knowledge of the Holy.* New York, NY: Harper & Row, 1961.

To learn more about Harvest House books and
to read sample chapters, log on to our website:

www.harvesthousepublishers.com

HARVEST HOUSE PUBLISHERS
EUGENE, OREGON